HR in the Corporate World The Unveiling of the Dark Side

By: HR Stories

Acknowledgments

I must acknowledge the contributions of many for the intricate tapestry that is my life. So many have sown seeds which have allowed me to grow and develop into the person that I now am. I now seek to return the favor and spread the seeds of experience for those who seek to know as I once did.

Dedication

Obviously, my life and purpose are deeply ingrained with the entanglements of my family and friends, but closest always to my heart are my children without whom I would not be subjected to the constant threat of the Baker Act.

A special dedication and thank to K.C. Boone wherever you are. Please know that without your persistence and belief in me, this book would still be a dream deferred. Years ago when I shared my dream with you, you never allowed me to forget about it. I miss you.

Foreword

This book is written not to bash corporations or my beloved HR profession. I only seek to unveil the dark side and offer solutions for improvement. Only when the truth is revealed can there be change.

As a lover of the HR profession, it is my belief that Human Resources is the true backbone of the company.

About The Author

HR Stories has over 17 years of professional HR experience working in various corporations in different HR roles from HR Recruiter to HR Manager to HR Director. HR Stories holds an AA in Business, BS in Social Welfare, and an MBA with a Specialization in Human Resources Management. HR Stories is HR certified.

Prior to a career change to the HR field, HR Stories was a legal assistant. Combined, HR Stories has over 30 years of working experience in the corporate environment.

Today, HR Stories is an Entrepreneur and HR consultant.

Table of Contents

Chapter 1 A Career In Human Resources Is A Splendid Opportunity
Chapter 2 The Realization
Chapter 3 Seen It All
Chapter 4 From A Place Of Knowing
Chapter 5 How did this Happen
Chapter 6 From A Place of Knowing
Chapter 7 Looking Back
Chapter 8 The Bright-Eyed Beginning
Chapter 9 Onward Still Believing
Chapter 10 Do As You Are Told
Chapter 11 When Doing the Right Thing Seems Wrong
Chapter 12 The Light Begins To Dawn
Chapter 13 The Glare Cannot Be Ignored
Chapter 14 Staring Me In The Face
Chapter 15 Will There Come A Time
Chapter 16 Management By Exception
Chapter 17 In The Face Of Overwhelming Evidence
Chapter 18 Seeking Justice Up The Ladder
Chapter 19 Do Unto Others As You Would Have Done Unto You
Chapter 20 Honor Those Whom You Depend Upon
Chapter 21 When All Else Fails
Chapter 22 In The Best Interest Of All Concerned
Chapter 23 Employee Satisfaction Pays Dividends
Chapter 24 Now What
Chapter 25 Options Reviewed
Chapter 26 Strategy Developed
Chapter 27 Plan Implemented
Chapter 28 Results Monitored
Chapter 29 Analysis Analyzed
Chapter 30 Remediation Recommended
Chapter 32 Responses Organized

Table of Contents-Cont'd

Chapter 33 New Plan Designed
Chapter 34 New Plan Implemented
Chapter 35 Results Seen
Chapter 36 Intrigued with Relief

For Whom This Book Is Written

Human resources professionals

To those who are tasked with a great deal of moral, ethical and legal responsibilities:

- You must put the human factor back in Human Resources by fostering and leading positive interactions and ethical decision making.
- You've chosen the profession therefore you must build respect, credibility and importance for the HR profession.
- You must stop being afraid to stand up for the core principles of the profession.
- Amongst many other tasks, you are also assigned the task of mediating solutions between management and subordinates. Both are important, neither is better than the other. Be impartial, fair and neutral and always seek to find amicable win-win solutions. Through you, employees' voices are heard. Be their voice and ensure fair and honest communication and treatment. Stand-up for injustice and stand your ground.
- Coach, develop and train supervisors, managers, and directors to do right by not only the organization, but by employees as well. Insist on fair and honest practices and when all else fails, don't be afraid to report unethical and/or unlawful acts.

Supervisors/Managers/Directors

You are not the whole, but are a part. No part is greater than the whole, but the whole exists because of the parts. Treat your parts well and they will repay you with excellent dividends. Treat your parts badly and they will also repay you with manifold dividends, but not the kind that you might find desirable.

Chapter 1 - A Career In Human Resources Is A Splendid Opportunity

My career path did not start in HR. A series of rather unpleasant workplace circumstances brought to my awareness the critical need for caring and ethical human resource professionals. I wanted to be a change agent, the kind of human resources professional that employees could feel comfortable with. I wanted to be an advocate for those who could not defend themselves. I saw a great injustice which became my mission maker.

Human resources offer a wonderful opportunity for employees to see both sides of the fence. Within the business, there operates an intricate system which is held up by a delicate balance of give and take. When the scales are tipped, the balance is lost and things go awry. Setting the scales aright is the job of the human resources professional. This can be very rewarding.

It has been a relatively short time since HR has hit the organizational spotlight as a much needed business partner. More and more businesses in all industries depend upon human resources professionals for recruiting, training, implementing HR standards/compliance, implementing and enforcing company policies and procedures, terminating, employee retention and satisfaction. This is a rapidly growing profession and opportunities are many.

Chapter 2 – The Realization

Let it be said that I do speak from experience. I have lost jobs and have suffered from the experiences. I, as a human resources professional do suffer job loss just like everyone else. There are no sacred cows in the pastures owned by corporations. Especially when you are a human resources professional who takes the HR code of moral and ethical values seriously.

Most lessons learned in business come from on the job and not from the college classroom. No college professor tells the whole truth about how the corporate environment really works. If you learn in college what I learned over the years, you would probably modify your career goals. But, the youngest among us feel that they can overcome any hurdles put before them. They are not easily deterred. This is a good thing and one which gives rise to the invincible achiever or so they think.

Human resources professionals are given a great deal of moral, ethical and legal responsibilities. In recruiting, training, reviewing, terminating and working with employees, there are a great deal of moral and ethical decisions to be made. These positive or negative consequences can have a huge impact on the business at large.

I have seen, from the inside, how human resources has transitioned from being the intermediary between employees and employers to the harbinger and facilitator of doom. Human resources is now the hiring/firing manager, who merely prepares the documentation to make things happen even if it's wrong. When a human resources professional attempts to uphold company policies/procedures and/or ethical standards, they themselves will experience backlash. Sadly, now it can be said that the human resources department is the revolving door of corporations.

Human resources professionals are not encouraged to find amicable and win/win solutions between workers and their supervisors or managers. With only the management team being right, the subordinate must take whatever he/she is given and like it or leave it. Solutions are the ones which end without litigation. It is rare and darn near nonexistent that employees actually get a fair hearing with just adjudication. No, this is not reality in the corporate world.

It is my belief that employee rights are a thing of the past. I make this statement, not out of bitterness, but as a factual observer. I have seen countless corporate mission statements which are not worth the paper on which they are printed. They boldly profess to treat employees fairly and with respect, never allowing retribution. I have worked for many different corporations and I know that these mission statements are merely for public show.

Most corporations claim to have a "zero tolerance" for harassment and retaliation. However, based on what I've witnessed firsthand, they actually have a "zero tolerance" for those who complain about these things. No matter how well intentioned at protecting employee rights the human resources professional maybe, if it is the desire of management to "get rid" of an employee because they complained, that human resources professional will be pressured and badgered until they have no choice but to "go along" with it and make sure it happens in a way that will protect the corporation. After all, we must maintain loyalty to our stakeholders.

A well know human resources agency tell us that a core value of human resources is to lead ethical values. Yet, it is a real challenge to realize this doctrine when the tables turn against you when attempting to ensure that decisions are fair and ethical and are implemented in an ethical manner.

Once upon a time long ago human resources was known as the personnel office. The role only handled employee paperwork and benefits. There was no real value or input coming from the personnel office. Today, human resources is said to be more strategic. We're told the mission of human resources changed to business partner. As a business partner, human resources must add value through various tasks that contribute to evolving a culture of corporate pride out of a culture of "every man for himself".

On an employee survey in 2016, one employee described human resources professionals as "extremely damaging people who use corporate law against the employees badly; always trying to filter people out with a crocodile smile...complete hypocrites who will assist sacking you and turn a blind eye to bad and bullying management .totally untrustworthy."

I am the first person to say that human resources professionals get a bad rap and that human resources is commonly misunderstood. I believe this is largely due to the fact that human resources professionals are the people employees see only when something goes wrong. Human resources professionals are there when someone gets fired, during exit interviews, disputes and almost every talk with human resources is behind closed doors. However, how employees perceive human resources outside the office door is a very good indicator as to how human resources connect to employees.

If employees are comfortable with HR, they will react openly and view us more favorably. The human resources professional who hides behind the HR office door and dares not enter the actual workplace for fear of running into employees will be treated with trepidation and opposition.

Chapter 3 – Seen It All

The things that I have witnessed would send shock waves through most corporations for they violate almost every policy so carefully written for public scrutiny. Because a policy is in writing does not in any way mean that it will be followed. Trust me on this for I know that truth of which I speak.

I do not base my judgment upon one or two circumstances, but upon many at many different organizations. It matters not the size of the organization or the internal make up of the organization. Rules are merely for "looks" and not for actions.

As any whistleblower knows, retaliation is very real. Why do you think that employee hotlines were set up in the first place? Employees are not so stupid as to believe that retaliation won't happen. The assurance of anonymity is the only reason that employees use hotlines.

With all of the whistleblower safety legislations and corporate policies against retaliation, why do you suppose that there still exists such verifiable retaliation as I personally have experienced? Just ask Edward Snowden had to leave his family and his country, in spite of assurances that whistleblowers are not to be subjected to retaliation. Do an internet search and see just a few of the many whistleblowers who have lost jobs, families, friends, etc., in direct retaliation for conscientiously reporting inappropriate behaviors.

I dare say that honesty is no longer the best policy, at least in my many experiences. I have watched high level human resources personnel knowingly try to sweep known policy violations under the proverbial "rug." They do not deal with the problem; they merely offer lip service and blame shifting. Often, it is the one who reports the abuse who gets abused. This is more common than even I had ever suspected, as I have since experienced.

Would you ever think that a human resources professional would hear such things as, I only want applicants from a particular zip code because the people are of a certain race or that they only want to see applications from white males; or that black applicants tend to have criminal histories. Regardless to whatever race or nationality you are, you should find blatant discriminatory and unlawful actions and comments offensive. Never could I ever imagine someone being bold enough to tell me, a HR professional to intentionally violate U.S. laws. Yet, over and over I have experience this boldness with which corporations allow inappropriate and illegal actions to go on day after day. They pretend to care, yet the proof is in the inaction.

Chapter 4 - From A Place Of Knowing

Workplace discrimination is real and retaliation is real. I know that these two things are forbidden by corporate policy manuals, even the law is against these things, yet corporations tolerated it and will even attempt to cover it up. How do I know these things? I have been on multiple occasions the victim of the actions of which I speak. I know firsthand that employees, regardless of the level on the corporate ladder, suffer all sorts of discrimination, abuse and retaliation.

Further, I have witnessed higher corporate level human resources personnel witnessing and allowing employee mistreatment. I have seen human resources professionals diligently work to cover up misconduct by management and additionally trumping up charges to get rid of the employee who dares to complain. Corporations have created an atmosphere of fear of losing their job. This tyrannical mindset keeps employee complaints to a minimum and keeps human resources professionals submissive.

I have witnessed the overt retaliation and outright slander of employees. I am aware of lies and manipulated write-ups to document the eventual termination of employees who would not keep quiet about unfair labor practices. Any whistleblower will tell you, news got out because the inside refused to do the right thing. For their honest efforts at correction, whistleblowers pay a very high price.

There are laws which are meant to protect whistleblowers and employees from retaliation. Those lofty sounding wordy policies and procedures, even when followed to the letter, offer no real avenue for support. Technically, the employee is on his/her own when filing a complaint. And if you expect the human resources department to help, you are in for a rude surprise. You won't receive help because they are too afraid to stand up for what's right – they are afraid that if they don't go along with the program, they themselves will face retaliation. I want to clarify, not all human resources professionals participate in unethical practices, but I've seen more than I care to think about who do. The days are long gone when human resource professionals were there to help and would go to bat for the employee. Those days have long since passed. Or, were they ever here? I can't recall a time at least not in my lifetime.

Human resources professional are used as the back up team to cover up abuse. They are the ones who provide the expertise in the development of documentation which portrays the victim as the wrong-doer. Talk about a magic trick. Human resources professionals are professionals indeed, especially when it comes to hiring and firing. Helping management "get the person out of the door" is how many spend their days in the HR office.

Chapter 5 – How did this Happen

But how did our jobs become so stressful? It's economies of scale; little monetary profits are realized from the HR department. Let the truth be told, the powers that be, see no real value in HR because to them, there is no clear indication how HR monetarily impact the bottom-line. So, the outcome is, one Human resources professional is cheaper than two or three and can do almost as much as four.

Often corporations have one human resources professional that supports up to 500 workers singlehandedly. To save on costs, the human resources professional is the entire HR department. You do everything. You multi-task, juggle priorities, learn the business, be a relationship builder, a mediator, solve conflicts, make sure employees are trained and developed, make sure it's a positive working environment, review terminations, conduct exit interviews, hire people, make sure performance reviews are done by the management team. You are the benefits person, the payroll person, the events person, and the investigator. Side note, the salary does not justify the workload. Sorry, I digress.

Far too often human resources professionals are pressured into making decisions that they are against. The fear of retaliation inhibits standing up for what's right and going against what's wrong. For those who do stand up, they are constructively discharged, asked to leave voluntarily or involuntarily terminated.

I caution that the human resources field is not for the weak at heart. It takes a strong individual to stand up for justice and do the right thing. The pressures of the role are more strenuous than any other position within the corporate environment. Telling one manager that they cannot write-up an employee simply because they "don't like them" or finding justifiable cause in an investigation can cause severe and sustain retaliatory actions either from employees themselves or management.

During my career when exercising my job duties as a human resources professional to implement HR standards and compliance, document discrimination, enforce company policies and procedures, or create a workplace free of the associated hostile environment, I was subjected to sustained retaliation. The ordinary human resources professional could not and would not endure what I've endured.

Standing firm and believing in doing the right thing, I have always prevailed even in the most difficult situations and against the largest of companies.

The truth is that the human resources field is a very lonely, cold-hearted, and extremely stressful world. If you are someone who likes to be liked by everyone and if you do not have a strong commitment to making the best ethical and moral decisions, and you're unable to take appropriate actions, well let's just say, HR is not the right job for you!

Chapter 6 – Looking Back

One of the great benefits of aging is the ability to look back and see with enhanced perspective. Once I was young and eager to make a difference in the world. Now, I realize that the impact of one person is not as great as I had imagined. A single person can change the world, but for the majority, our steps go largely unnoticed.

It is from this experienced perspective that I now sit and reflect upon the overall line of truths exposed within the highs and lows of working in the human resources field. There is a pattern revealed which is the major reason I am writing this book. I want everyone to be aware. I desire to share my experiences in hopes that someone will learn from those experiences. The lessons I learned were often difficult, yet I persevered and continued to take the next step toward the goals that I set for myself.

With great forethought and determination, I set my sights upon lofty goals and I gave my best efforts toward attainment. It was not until long into the process that I realized that it was all set forth in the beginning and I am merely the experiences of the exercise instead of the determinant of the course.

When I entered the HR field, I had certain expectations based upon the teachings of my parents. I was taught that we should always be honest and truthful at all times. I was taught that lying is bad and that we will surely be punished for the wrong that we do.

But, my experience in HR taught me different things. It taught me that wrong-doers are not always punished. It taught me life is not always fair. It taught me that hard work does not always pay. It taught me that much of what I was taught is simply not true.

This book is a testament to the facts of HR, at least as I have experienced them. I do believe that, regardless of the consequences, the truth shall always set me free. Indeed, I have firsthand knowledge that this is true. And I have the experience to know that the truth is not always appreciated and can have some nasty consequences. Often the world prefers that the truth not be told, especially that it be kept hidden. It is not always necessary to lie, but surely it is most often desirable that the truth be hidden.

The hiding of the truth, I find, is a major tenet of how the world really operates. Whether in a court of law or in a corporate boardroom, the truth is typically least desirable when the facts are not on the side of right.

I once believed that at the heart of all businesses was the sincere desire to be honest and provide for the welfare of the employees. The sad reality is typically the opposite. Now that the Supreme Court has granted "human" status to corporations, actual humans have a tough time gaining the same rights as corporations.

We have sat and allowed our rights to be melted away while corporate lawyers and lobbyists have worked diligently to enhance corporate rights. As the saying goes, "Why close the barn door after the cows are out?" The cows have long since left the barn and now we are awakening to the facts of current business life.

My experiences are not exclusive, but are rather indicative of the current daily workings of corporations worldwide. I thought human resources to be an esteemed position of fairness between the business and its employees, however, it seems that the function of human resources is merely to expedite the demise of employee rights and job satisfaction and uphold the wrongdoing of the corporation and the management team it employ.

As the years have passed, I have watched not only employees lose their rights and favored status; I have witnessed firsthand the abuses by corporate managers who are allowed with corporate approval to operate without oversight or legal controls.

Employee rights is almost an oxymoron now. Employees have the right to do what they are told and to not question authority. Customers are allowed to abuse employees and employees are further insulted with abuse from managers. Bullying is a well-known well-researched problem, yet there are no laws in place to protect employees. "At-will" really means the company can abuse and mistreat employees at there will with no consequences.

How have we as humans but more importantly, as human resources professionals and advocates for justice allowed this to happen? Why so much apathy and indifference?
I am a firm believer in humanity and our ability to do what is needed to succeed. I have been in many seemingly hopeless situations, yet I always get up and take the next step forward. This attitude, I believe, is part of the nature of humanity. You need humanity to awaken you to the harsh realities of the profession and only then will you be able to be a true advocate for the human resources profession.

I have seen enough from the inside to know how things really work in the corporate world. From this experience, I seek to awaken you to this reality and offer you my best attempt at problem resolution. From the top to the bottom, there exists dissatisfaction with the current corporate environment. Only those who are at the very top, the real owners, benefit from the current system.

We've obviously got work to do, but let's first take a short walk down memory lane to see where we are and how we got here.

Chapter 7 – The Bright-Eyed Beginning

I, like most young people, began my working life with wide eyes of wonder. I just knew I could change the world by making my contribution. I was idealistic and enthusiastic. Even today, these qualities are held within, even if not so openly displayed.

I graduated high school at the tender age of 16 and off to college I went ready to conquer the world or at least I thought. Reality and life prevailed and I eventually dropped out due to the overwhelming demand of college life.

I eventually got married and luckily for me my husband had a career earning great wages that afforded me the opportunity to be a housewife and a stay-at-home mom. Of course, being the constant overachiever boredom encouraged my movement into the workforce.

My first real job came through a training program I attended. Back then training programs and opportunities were readily available to underemployed individuals and I took full advantage of this opportunity. Due to my great organization skills and my ability to type really fast, I was honored in the newspaper for the county's fastest typist. This ultimately landed me two job offers with two well known and highly reputable agencies.

Eventually, I worked my way through the system and landed a job as a legal secretary with a well known agency. It was here that my desire to purse human resources as a profession was formed.

Let me share with you the situation that ultimately changed my life:

As I mentioned earlier, I was a legal assistant. I worked with an attorney who misused me and my skills. This attorney forced me to research, write and type all of his legal motions and pleadings. When I shared with him my discontent, his response was that "I have good writing skills and that I was "attorney like" and he continued with this unethical practice.

Utilizing the company's complaint process, I complained to management. One day the manager over the department called me into a meeting along with the corporate human resources director. During this meeting the department manager proceeded to tell me in these exact words - very rudely, *"Who do you think you are – you're a nobody - you're just an assistant -just do as you're told because if you don't we will terminate you for complaining."*

This one-way conversation was held in the presence of the corporate human resources director. Not only did she allow the department manager to berate and devalued me, but she did not stop the attorney from forcing me to do his work.

This unfortunate or as I look at it now, this fortunate experience changed my life forever. The very next day I reenrolled in college with two goals in mind. First, to equip myself with education and knowledge and secondly, I wanted to pursue a career in HR so that I could be the type of human resources professional who advocates integrity, justice, impartiality, and fairness for all.

Luckily for me the damaging words that were meant to disarm me actually lit a fire within me, but what about those employees who don't have the same fortitude? While this experience was more than 25 years ago, the point I'm making is that fast forward many years later, human resources professionals still operate with the same apathy and indifference.

Chapter 8 – Onward Still Believing

On the climb up the corporate ladder, everyone takes a few hits. There are minor setbacks which are fairly easy to overcome. At the lower levels, the hits are not as devastating, partly because of the resilience of youth and partly because of the position toward the bottom of the ladder.

Why do we continue to believe in a field where there is so much pressure to support the organization even when they are wrong? What is it that keeps us in the game? The realization that we are not just cogs in the wheel should give us enough strength to cut our losses and step out in the name of ethics. What are we afraid of?

Perhaps it is our so called esteemed human resources experts who tell us to follow the leaders and do as we are told and corporate bosses who reaffirm this concept. Thinking for ourselves is less and less rewarded. It seems that we are constantly told go to work and don't make waves. They say HR has the power to make a difference, yet we are not empowered to make a difference. Has the organization failed us, have we fallen into the trap of the corporate bosses or have we failed ourselves?

There seems to be a common thread among all businesses. Regardless of which corporate door you enter, the environment and tactics seem very much alike. Was this purposefully created to keep human resources professionals like worker bees, in check? Or did it just happen because we've allowed it?

I wish someone would survey human resources professionals and ask them if they've ever felt pressure to go along with the program. If many of them tell the truth, we would find out that most have. Yet, the intrepid warrior lives to survive another day, always seeking to find a way, all in hopes of keeping a job.

Chapter 9 - Do As You Are Told

What happens when the human resources professional investigate and reports wrong-doing to their superiors and they are told to "do as you are told?" This surely happens all too often. This presents quite the pickle for the conscientious human resources professional.

Human resources professionals are obligated to do something about known wrong-doing, but they get in trouble if they do. Not a fun place to be. The right thing to do is to stop all inappropriate actions. But when you do, just make sure you're ready for what will eventually come – retaliation. It WILL HAPPEN.

No one likes to be found out, so people will be furious with you. Granted, they did wrong, but you'll find out who's the boss when you put them under the lamp of scrutiny.

Chapter 10 - Advocates for Justice

Bullying is common in today's society. It's no wonder that it makes it way in to businesses. It seems that bully managers/supervisors/directors are highly esteemed by those above them while they are reviled by those below them. Human resources professionals who are aware of bully management behaviors and do nothing are accessories after the fact.

Policies against hostile working environments do little to stop known abuses. Having witnessed and experienced firsthand bullying by managers/supervisors/directors, I know that little if anything is done to correct abusive behaviors. One would think that once discovered some type of corrective action would follow. However, this is all too often not the case. Creating and maintaining an atmosphere of fear seems to be the desire of most corporations. Fear is used as the greatest tool to get employees to do what you want them to do.

Bullying behavior is a form of abuse. Bully managers/supervisors/directors do untold damage to the productivity of employees. Working in a stressful environment can be the downfall of an otherwise good employee. How bullying affects a person depends upon the person, but typically its effects are always negative. No one likes to be yelled at or criticized mercilessly. Belittling and berating employees creates an environment in which there builds great animosity and hatred.

These bullied employees are the very ones who will represent you to your customers or worse, they tell their family and friends. What do you suppose will be their message and how will it be conveyed? Employees who are otherwise powerless will find all sorts of ways to get even with ruthless bosses. You'll wonder why your sales are down, but won't connect the dots to the real reason. Absenteeism rates will sour high. Recruiting costs will increase due to high turnover. Employee dissatisfaction costs and it costs a lot. You would do yourself a favor to realize this and remedy any abusive situations that come to your attention.

Human resources professionals are in the business of ensuring good working environments. If human resources professional do nothing about known bullying behaviors, what does this say about the human resources professional? If human resources professionals seem to join with the bullies to further bully employees, then what is the point of having them around? Human resources professionals must regain focus on their actual intended purpose within the organization. Human resources professionals are to be advocates for justice, yet seldom is this the case.

Chapter 11- Thorny HR Predicaments

Human resources professionals are given a great deal of moral, ethical and legal responsibilities. So what should one do when a hiring manager tells the human resources professional that he/she only wants to hire males, white people, or young people? Ding, ding, ding, the bells in your head must sound loudly. Remember, human resources professionals are advocates for moral and ethical standards. Yet, so many human resources professionals are reluctant to stop unethical practices. Even worse, they themselves participate in unethical practices.

In no organizational structure should HR ever report to anyone other than the highest ranking official. This might help to alleviate the ruthless pressures faced by human resources professionals to "go along" with the program or to find "innovative solutions" to support management's unethical requests.

I know of one company where the human resources professional role reported to a lower level store manager. The store manager mistreated employees, unjustifiably wrote them up, and retaliated against employees if they complained. So many lawsuits were field against that particular location until corporate headquarters had no choice but to send in a team of other human resources professionals to investigate. When the human resources professional was questioned about why she allowed such occurrences, the response was, fear of retaliation.

This type of structure undoubtedly produces a conflict of interest. It prevents the human resources professional from keeping an objective outlook on situations. When human resources professionals are subjected to the demands of lower ranking management, the human resources professional is completely ineffective.

As it is often said, "Hope springs eternal." Always there is hope, and we should cling to hope if all else is lost. The interconnectedness of our work is real. Human resources professionals are valuable for their expertise, but there decidedly comes a point of diminishing returns. When the cost of mistreatment is seen as greater than the human resources professional's contribution to the bottom line, then HR is sacrificed for the good of the whole.

One unethical manager can cost a company millions. Yet, this is seen as an acceptable risk by most companies. Everyone loses in the long run.

Chapter 12 - When Doing The Right Thing Seems Wrong

Sometimes doing the right thing is wrong in everyone's eyes. Human resources professionals are often placed in a situation where they question moral and ethical values of others, but they must also question their own moral and ethical values. Should I step in and stop inappropriate behavior? Should I report my findings of wrong-doing or shouldn't I?

Often, human resources professionals are retaliated against if they do what's right and more times than not they give in to the pressures of not doing the right thing for this very reason. Fear of suffering through retaliation and fear of losing one's job is a great motivator.

In order to escape accountability for their actions, managers do everything in their power to promote their own agenda. They use secrecy and silence as their first line of defense. If secrecy fails, the manager attacks the credibility of the human resources professional. If they cannot silence the human resources professional then every attempt is made to make sure that no one believes them. To this end, they will marshal an impressive array of arguments, from the most blatant denial to the most sophisticated and elegant rationalization. The human resources professional is not a team player, the human resources professional does not know how to build relationships, the human resources professional is not a partner, the human resources professional does not understand the business needs.

If you blow the whistle, get ready for the retaliation that always follows. Honesty, it seems, is no longer desired nor beneficially rewarded.

So, why even bother? Why do some honest human resources professionals still feel compelled to honor their sense of obligation to tell the truth and to expose inappropriate behavior?

Even when they know that retaliation will follow, a truly honest human resources professional will stand up and do what's right.

We are taught in childhood that we should tell the truth and do what is morally right. Yet, in HR, we spend our days living through myriad examples of how this gets us into trouble. It's one of life's greatest Catch-22's.

People are more prone to self-preservation and will usually go out further on a limb to save themselves than others. It is often noted that whistleblowers speak up after they are terminated, yet no one ever mentions what they did and why the termination was actually retaliation for truth telling beforehand. It was the truth that eventually did "set them free" from their employment.

You would think that any really smart corporate head would want to know if something is going on to jeopardize the corporation. Yet, the evidence in fact proves otherwise. Often, it is at the highest corporate levels that inappropriate behavior originates. As the layers of the Enron scandal unraveled, it was seen how the top managers were the ones calling the inappropriate shots.

As the slang saying goes, "No one likes a narc." Another favorite is, "Snitches get stitches." Why do we not appreciate human resources professionals who tell the truth rather than vilify them, especially if they are trying to help you avoid costly lawsuits? It seems rather obvious that a good human resources professional is less desirable than a bad one, yet bad human resources professional's cost much more in the long run.

Chapter 13 – The Light Begins To Dawn

How many times do you have to be hit in the head before you get the message? Apparently, quite a few, given the fact that we all have to make a living and support our families. So, as you go from organization to organization each time you soften your stance.

As the years roll by and time takes its toll, I began to see a pattern develop. I noticed that with each organizational move, my role as a human resources professional was the same from company to company. Surely, even the least educated person can see that this has been done by deliberate design. The downfall of the human resources profession at the same time cannot happen except by the intent of the most powerful people in the company.

High HR turnover is a very good indicator that there is a function disconnect within an organization. As a general rule, happy or at least satisfied HR people do not leave their current employment. It is human nature to avoid change.

So, what is it that causes so many human resources professionals to job hop? Most human resources professionals have to be caught in untenable situations in order to resort to changing jobs. Learning a new company is not a lot of fun. Walking into a new environment can be exciting or terribly frightening for some.

So, are we examining the problem from too far down the rabbit hole to see the reality of the situation from any angle? Perhaps, but on the level that we can see, we see that things just aren't what we would previously refer to as "right." The dominos seem to be falling in a downward pattern. How is this possible? How does HR escape the forces totally beyond his/her control?

I believe that the power of one can change the world, just as I did in the ignorance of my youth. I do believe also that the power of two can make changes twice as fast. Obviously, the more the merrier. Things can be corrected, but the average human resources professional must make it his/her business to restore our profession, The apathetic mindset which allowed us to not be minding the mint must be changed. We must demand that our high esteemed positions be restored. All power belongs to us, but we must use our power to bring about the desired changes. Make no mistake, I understand the apathy. Fear of retaliation is real (but we'll discuss this a little later).

On the level of one corporate human resources professional, a microcosm can be seen which reflects the whole. More and more, individual rights have been taken away. What used to be considered normal benefits for every employee, insurance and retirement plans are falling by the wayside. With each passing year, benefits are lost at staggering rates. Now that the Affordable Care Act is in place, the most damaging effects to today's society is experienced.

With wages at the lowest in modern times, current employees are faced with staggering insurance premiums which cause many to have to decide between premiums and groceries. Today's workers are already strapped, now another blow is felt. This one may be the cathartic one which breaks the camel's back.

People will only tolerate so much abuse. When people feel otherwise hopeless, they will resort to survival instincts and will do whatever is necessary to feed themselves and their families. We have watched this happen during the Arab Spring and other such movements. When people have no other choice, they will take action. Again, I digress.

Chapter 14 – The Glare Cannot Be Ignored

Take a man, down on his luck and you will see what he is made of. He will either lift himself up or he will give up completely. Never one to admit defeat, I always pick myself up and justify taking the next step. Choosing always to look forward rather than backward, I seek always to overcome my adversities and to learn from each of them. Life will offer you some unpleasant things, but for those who choose to continue to fight, life can offer some grand rewards.

Life was never meant to be all roses and no thorns. With the good comes the bad, as we've all been taught. I have no unreasonable expectations. I realize that everything is a matter of perspective and perception. No two people see things the same, so there will always be grounds for conflict. The conflicts are not in question, it is the resolutions which seem to be lacking. Why is it so difficult for two people, on the same team, to find amicable solutions to problems – for the benefit of the entire team?

There is no "I" in team, we are told. Yet, much of the corporate dissonance comes from the egotistical "I" perspective. When does a manager take priority over all of his/her subordinates? When does pride really offer the best possible option? As with all of life, pride does come before a fall. Sadly, the pride of one can cause the fall of many. I've seen this over and over. Managers who are more concerned with their own agenda and human resources professionals who allow them to carry on with the antic. In reality who should we blame?

Chapter 15 – Staring Me In The Face

You get up in the morning and hope for the best. No one gets up seeking the worst. How long before your day starts before you have to face negativity? Was the negativity of your own creation or was it imposed upon you? How were you affected by the negativity? Did you let it ruin the rest of your day? Too many times, the least little thing can cause the next several hours to be filled with discontent for yourself and others. Why do we punish ourselves and others?

If, like me, you live in the big city, traffic is not for the meek and faint-hearted. Traffic is brutal, exemplifying the "dog-eat-dog" mentality. Trust me when I say that road rage is real and happens for a reason. Day after day of this seemingly relentless brutality does take its toll. By the time you get to work, you are already loaded for bear. How many are wise enough to take a step back and start fresh at the office door?

Unfortunately for most human resources professionals there's no such thing as taking a step back to refresh. Challenges and opportunities meet you at the door constantly. We are always putting out a fire and typically one that could have been prevented if only management listened to HR recommendations in the first place.

I've come to realize that human resources professionals are in place not because companies want to protect themselves from liability. Theoretically HR has come a long way from the days of "the personnel office", and now it's thought to be "more strategic", yet, the fact of the matter is, management is unconcerned about following rules and regulations and/or HR recommendations. They continue to see HR as the department that "handles the paperwork". Ultimately, human resources professionals are pressured into going along with the status quo.

My experience has taught me that there are two types of human resources professionals: those who shut-up and follow the script and those who don't. I've personally witnessed human resources professionals who "willed" themselves to turn the other way and allow inappropriate actions to occur. Again, I am not ignorant to the fears of retaliation. I've been on the receiving end more times than I'd like to remember so I definitely know how it feels.

Chapter 16 - Will There Come A Time

Will there come again a time when all players on the team are team oriented? In the game of big business, it seems that there are all sorts of divisions and striations. I am reminded of the "divide and conquer" rule of warfare. The Bible says that "a house divided cannot stand." (Matt 12:25) This is ancient wisdom and down to earth common sense. Why then do corporations seem to set HR to fail?

The obvious divisions within the corporate structures create all sorts of avenues for divisive splits and destructive behaviors. When the management team and human resources professional cannot seem to work together, does not the entire organization suffers? And who is tasked with keeping the peace between the two and why do they not do so? In truth, there seems to be an almost literal division between the employers and the employees.

When every decision is made for the benefit of the company regardless of the consequences for the employees, it must be realized that there will be unpleasant consequences, typically for the entire organization. Off hand, I do not have accurate statistics for support, but I do believe based on my experience that internal conflicts seem to be getting more and more frequent. There seems to exist an atmosphere of discontent underlying the general business front-face.

When you go into a company and it's a toxic environment. All you see are sad faces on employees, or worse mad faces then it's a safe bet that there is some tyrannical managerial operative working behind the scenes. You don't have to be a genius to realize that an employee's behavior and facial expressions tell a story. Think about how you behave when you are stressed or sad or mad. Employees are human and we need to remember this above all else.

Corporate policies set the tone for the organization, even if they are not followed. Just as retaliation is forbidden in the corporate by-laws, it happens and it happens frequently. It happens in governmental organizations and non-governmental organizations. Policies do offer at least one leg to stand on when an employee is left with no other choice but to take their case to court. I really don't think there ever was an employee who just went to court for the fun of it. I think a person really has to feel court is their last resort before they go to the trouble of filing suit.

Often times lawsuits are filed because people feel abused and that a grave injustice was done to them. In many cases lawsuits can be avoided if only someone takes the time to listen. Most employees work diligently within the company system following requisite HR protocols to resolve the issues. All attempts at reasonable resolution fail and they are left with no other alternatives but to reach out to the courts as a course of last resort.

Human resources professionals must dissolve conflicts before they get to the stage of lawsuits. Any conflict can be handled by reasonable people if they are determined and willing to do the right thing. There need be no ugliness or insults. All conflicts can be resolved by peaceful means. Of this I am convinced. But, it takes a willingness to admit that a wrong has been done, if in fact it has been. Many times, conflict comes merely from perceptual differences.

Because an employee feels insulted does not mean that there was such intended action by the employer. Yes, there are far too many times when employees are insulted purposefully and then when confronted, the employer lies. Of course, the story can go both ways and no employee is perfect either. But, again let me state for the record, I do believe that conflict resolution is the backbone of HR. It is this that we must realize and master.

The overworked human resources professional would have to work less if turnover were less. Consider this when you are faced with the unpleasant task of listening to one more story about an abused employee. Perhaps it is in your best interest to retain employees, if at all possible. Take a few minutes and help the employee realize that the organization values him/her and is willing to resolve differences if at all possible.

Consider the volume of paperwork involved in firing someone and then hiring someone else. You know, that the next person will not be trained, so you will have to go through the training process as well. Really, we need to take better care of the employees in which we have already invested so much into. So, in a sense, we determine our own fates. A shortcut here can be costly there.

Before the problem escalates, there must be a cooperative environment between the management team and the human resources professional. The management team must also realize the high cost of turnover. When there is conflict between these two, entities everyone loses. There should never be allowed conflict between these two positions. There must be cooperation and respect between those who are in charge of the organizations human resources.

Chapter 17 - Management by Exception

You have surely heard of management by exception. It is human nature, given the constant pressures to succeed at all costs, to take the path of least resistance. When accomplishments far outnumber the failures, it is common practice to focus only on the things which need to be corrected. The exceptions become the focus and seem to take over the entire energy of the organization. If it ain't broke, don't fix it. Why bother with the things that work. Focus on the things that are broken.

The management by exception mentality creates an environment in which only criticisms are heard and appreciation is seldom acknowledged. Make one mistake and the whole organization seems to know about it. Make the highest sales or produce great quality work and few people know about it. This is typical in today's overworked overstressed work places. Just to get the doors open and keep the place running seems to require everyone's full attention. Improvements are had at the expense of something else. Fix one thing and another thing breaks. Or, just don't fix anything at all.

Is it any wonder that today's human resources professional is stressed just like all the other employees? The human resources professional is typically caught in a rock and a hard place and a no-win situation. Neither the bosses nor the employees are happy with things as they currently are. Burnout is very prevalent. Turnover is very high in spite of the huge unemployment numbers. What pushes employees to quit even if they have little hope of finding another job?

Everyone has limits. Sometimes the demands are more than a human can bear. Remember, people don't just live for work. They work to live. There are families to feed and responsibilities to take care of. If the plumbing breaks, who will give you time off with pay to get that fixed? If your children are sick, who needs not worry about taking some time off to nurse the child back to health? There are workers who have real life problems and are often forced to choose between work and family and the struggle to choose work is more often encouraged rather than discouraged. This should never be, but unfortunately many employees and their families do suffer needlessly. Ultimately, who really does pay the price?

A commitment to helping employees make the balance of work and home responsibilities a little easier would lead to mutual benefits. Employees who are better able to balance the demands on their time are more satisfied and content. This in turns leads to real benefits for the company in terms of competitive advantage, productivity gains, lower turnover rate, and employee loyalty.

Yes, there are those who do take advantage. I remember the employee whose grandmother died three times in the same year, or so he told. The bad apples do spoil it for the masses. But, there are those who are hard working honest people who simply need to be supported in their time of crisis. These are the ones who often come to my mind when I think that I can't take one more minute of this job.

I do this for those who need me. We are in this together and when they simply need someone to listen, I always try to be there to offer whatever comfort I can. The human resources profession is about more than just hiring and firing. I believe that humans need organizational support and I do my very best to provide all that I can even when corporate directives tells me otherwise.

I watch as a person who can barely read suffers with an application for insurance. I see those who barely speak the language are too shy to ask for help. I watch the pain of those going through life's traumatic events, such as the loss of a loved one and I must offer my assistance and comfort. Remember, HR is about humans and humans being human.

Human resources professionals have lost touch with their humanity as the need to keep a job has replaced ensuring fair human to human interaction. I sit in judgment of people based solely on a resume day after day. How can any one person be reduced to one piece of paper? But, there's just not enough time, is our excuse. Typically, a candidate is picked based on a page full of words and all the others are dumped without even a fighting chance to be seen or heard. This is what has been done to today's HR departments. No longer are we concerned about meeting face to face – we hide behind computer screens and savor our anonymity. The latest trend is telephone interviewing. We conduct telephone interviews because we don't have time or we don't want to take the time to bring people in or what I have seen recently we use this method to weed certain groups of people out. No more face-to-face interaction as days gone past.

I dare say that one short cut creates another. If HR takes a shortcut in hiring, then the person hired will take similar shortcuts while working. Distance creates a system in which people tend to feel less responsible. Just like in a classroom, if the teacher fails to acknowledge the students, the students feel like they can take advantage of their anonymity. In those classrooms where the teacher has her eye on everyone, there are few who try to take advantage. People who feel noticed and appreciated are more likely to return the favor.

The competition between employer and employee has caused great damage which now must be repaired. The coming together of both, with the assistance of the human resources professional, makes for an overall better working environment and surely a more prosperous one. How anyone can believe that heartless organizations with huge turnover can really be prosperous is shocking. This really defies logic and common sense, but they still believe it.

Returning our businesses to places with human compassion is the answer to fixing our economic problems. An employee who is well treated performs well. This is basic business sense. Think about how you feel at work and how your performance mirrors how you are treated. I know that when I am treated badly, I am upset and cannot perform my best. We are humans and we are affected by the way others treat us, just as others are affected by the way we treat them. It all goes hand and hand.

I understand that we can't run a Willy Wonka© type factory, but we can very easily begin to treat our most valuable assets with respect and appreciation. When a five year award is a plastic water bottle or plastic pen, and this is an example of a company that still gives tenure awards, we've gone off the path of common business sense. When a five year employee deserves no more than a dollar water bottle, we can no longer blame employees for being disloyal. This is an absolute disgrace especially when it is a million or billon dollar company.

I can personally attest to the fact that employees are treated as less valuable than cash assets. Many managers today do not equate the cost of hiring and turnover to be part of the cost of doing business. They disregard the "problematic" employee, who has been trained and has worked diligently for the organization for many years, and simply get rid of the troublemaker. It has become easier to get rid of employees and get new ones than to try to work out problems and differences.

Bringing on a new employee involves understanding the intricate details of jobs being filled and the requirements for the job. Then there's finding prospective employees, designing the interview process and seeing to standards being in place that hopefully leads to the right person being hired for the job. Once hired, HR must see to the employee's well being by working benefits and work condition issues in hopes of retaining valuable personnel to ensure the company's ability to provide quality goods and services. HR also ensures that ample and effective training is available and completed to increase flexibility and productivity of the workforce for the company's survivability in the competitive global marketplace.

The lost knowledge is not regained by simply hiring a new employee. The new employee knows nothing about the business and must go through the tedious training process at great expense. How much business is lost while the new employee is trained? Could a simple solution have avoided this situation entirely? Managers today rather enjoy having lots of new employees because the ego driven manager likes to be the center of attention. Poorly trained managers don't like to be questioned and they like to lord over the minions so that they will feel powerful.

These egotistical managers never last for very long and they have to be replaced. Does this cost the organization? It costs a great deal. Low morale is a major business killer. Who wants to sell for the one who screams at you? Who cares about customers when you are about to lose your job? How do we expect stressed out employees to offer us their best service? This just makes no sense – to anyone. But, this behavior goes on day after day, week after week, year after year.

In order to avoid going to court, many organizations now utilize arbitration to resolve differences. Could this be a possible solution for lowering turnover and improving satisfaction? The pretend problem resolution conferences now held are bogus and aren't really about resolution so much as sweeping the problem under the rug. These "resolved" problems will and do resurface. A real solution requires agreement between both parties. There must be a truly amicable attempt to bring both sides to a common ground.

It is only when the integrative and ongoing nature of corporations commitment is to provide employees fair and equitable treatment. When policy implications are intended to establish a way where all employees can feel a part of the organization. When managers and employees can communicate effectively with each other, and when rules are fair and just. That real change can be seen.

Human resources professionals have been put in an awkward position, we are no longer allowed to truly go to bat for the employees. We can't even go to bat for ourselves if truth be told. We have no more rights to fair treatment than do all other employees. Those who sincerely seek fairness are typically found guilty of some trumped up charges and are dismissed. If a human resources professional is so treated, do other employees even stand a chance?

It must be stated that honesty in the workplace is at an all time low. When managers and employees lie to cover their actions with such disregard for the truth or fairness, there must be a total breakdown of the system. And allow me to say, the system is broken. I can vouch for that based upon my own experiences.

How can a fair system of arbitration be put in place? There would have to be objective parties making the final decisions. Is there such a thing as a truly fair hearing? With the confidentiality concerns, who can really hear the case? Once upon a time, the human resources professional was the person who heard the case. Now, the human resources professional may have a case of his/her own against the corporation.

Chapter 18 – In The Face Of Overwhelming Evidence

How many of us really overlook the obvious? Did you see the axe coming? Were you aware of the rumors about layoffs? Did you see the dots being connected with each passing day? Or were you simply oblivious to all that goes on around you?

Many people, after the fact, reflect and realize that the truth was staring them in the face, but they didn't really want to see what was clearly evident. Granted, there are layoffs and closures which have been done rather ruthlessly without any such warning signs. Employees called in on a Sunday afternoon and told to clean out their desk and to not report back for work, ever, actually happened. More than once, in fact.

Advance notice gives workers some transition time to adjust to the prospective loss of employment, to seek and obtain other jobs, and, if necessary, to enter skill training or retraining that will allow these workers to compete successfully in the job market. Yet, most companies that I've experienced do everything in their power to go around this law. They lay off a little at a time or use other tactics.

This I find inhuman and disgraceful. There is no reason to treat your fellow human beings with such disregard and callousness. Granted, the losing of a job is devastating. But losing a job without any forewarning is far more hurtful.

It has been said that losing a job is much like a death in the family. For me, I do believe this is true. Certainly not for everyone, but for those who have invested their best into a company which returns their hard work with total disdain, typically a depression ensues. Often times, marriages fail under the strain of job loss and the devastating effects.

Chapter 19 - Seeking Justice Up The Ladder

Employees including Human resources professionals are told that if they do not agree with the decision, they can appeal to higher levels in search of fairness. Let me state for the record that all persons up the ladder work for the same people as the ones who prompted you to seek justice in the first place, and they will side with the corporation – always, because they have corporate people over them. No corporation seeks to settle differences by siding against the corporation. Oh, Johnny was unfairly treated so we'll just give him a bonus for the mistreatment. It will never happen.

Now, Johnny gets a lawyer and the situation changes. Now, Johnny gets lots of attention and pretend concern. Every effort will now be made to smooth over Johnny's complaint. Johnny will probably have to go to court, but Johnny will now have a chance at restitution. All of this could have been avoided if Johnny had simply been given the apology he thought he was due.

Most whistleblowers don't just one day decide to blow the whistle to outsiders. They typically follow the chain of command and report the perceived wrongdoing out of conscience. What they seek is for the organization to mend its wicked ways. Once the organization becomes aware that someone is one to their wicked ways, the whistleblower is soon harassed and terminated under false pretenses. It is then that the whistleblower lets the world know what goes on behind closed doors. This need not be.

It would seem more reasonable to me to appreciate those who bring corruption to the awareness of the bosses. This demonstrates ethics and honor, which should be valuable to any organization. Yet, the opposite happens and the honorable employee is vilified and terrorized till they either quit or are terminated. All whistleblowers suffer – this is fact. Just ask

Edward Snowden who recently sought asylum in Russia. Imagine having to go to Russia to escape America. What's wrong with this picture?

Chapter 20 - Do Unto Others As You Would Have Done Unto You

When we realize that happy employees make for happy managers, we all benefit. There will never come a day when unhappy employees will make for happy customers. So, we must do our best to put smiles on employee's faces so that they will, in turn put smiles on customer's faces.

It does not take much to offer a kind gesture to another. Does it cost you anything to say hello to an employee who passes you? Don't you like seeing smiling faces? Why should others receive less? Taking the temperature of an organization is rather simple. You do not need elaborate surveys or focus groups. Just take a few minutes to watch your employees. Their actions speak volumes about the place they work.

If you see the majority of employees looking totally stressed out, then something awful lurks in managerial garb. If you see employees totally slacking and relaxed with managers totally stressed, you might need to work on delegation skills. Human resources professionals have offices in order to protect confidentiality. Offices are not provided as a barrier to keep the evil employees away. Let the walls come down and walk among the peoples.

How the employees react to the management team and HR outside the office door is a very good indicator as to how the management and HR relates to employees. If employees are comfortable with the management and HR, they will react openly and forthcoming. The manager and/or Human resources professional who hide behind the office door and dare not enter the actual workplace for fear of running into employees will be treated with trepidation and opposition. If employees shy away from management and/or HR, then you must surely know you have an organizational problem which must be corrected.

When the very people who are in the organization to interact with employees is not seen as trustworthy by employees, then red flags should be flying high. It has been my experience that employees, when they do not feel threatened, will typically be open and honest about how they feel. When they feel threatened, they will say little and lie if need be. How can a business operate well when employees must work in so stressful an environment? Do you work well under stress?

Have you ever tried random one-on-one impromptu employee chats? Have you ever sat down and tried to learn even one skill on the work floor? Have you ever asked an employee if they would like to host an employee meeting? There are so many ways to open up dialogues with employees, if you are willing to take a few minutes out of your "way-too-busy-for-bothersome-employees" schedule.

What if employees had the positional power that you have and could treat you the way you treat them? This would be quite eye-opening for those who use their powerful positions to reign supreme over others. Have you ever considered that employees have their own forms of power to wield over the managers? You would be wise to open your eyes and see the reality of who actually drives the business.

Chapter 21 - Honor Those Whom You Depend Upon

Consider who butters your bread: Is it the corporation or those who make up the corporation? Whom do you really serve? This is not the same as whom do you answer to, as you might at first think. Peeling away the corporate layers reveals the reality of the corporate structure and shows that the majority of all corporations are employee based. Just like America, the citizens make the country not the other way around.

It should be an honor to represent the employees who allow you to know their secrets and have some sort of control over their lives. You have a great responsibility and should take it very seriously. It should not be seen as a burden, but should be considered an honor. Having the ability to change a person's life must be held in high regard. Your actions are not without grave consequences. You have the ability to cause a person to feel devastated or appreciated.

Were there no employees, you would not have a job. If you go to work each day with this at the forefront of your mind, then perhaps you will be able to offer a better daily experience to those with whom you interact. You are not hired to merely exist. You are hired to represent the company and the employees. How you see your part in the structure may make all the difference. See your role as critical to the success of the organization and always do your best to bridge the gap between employers and employees.

Over time, you may get jaded and feel hopeless in your efforts. You are not alone if you have ever felt this way. Employees often feel the same way. Imagine going to work each day, making the widgets hour after hour. What about this makes you feel valued and appreciated? Yes, you will get paid, but life is about more than just a paycheck. How you feel daily determines how many widgets and the quality of the widgets that you make.

Like the a famous say goes, "walk a mile in the other person's shoes. Then you can truly understand how they feel".

Have you ever really considered what separates you from the workers on the floor? Is it merely an education? Is it ambition? Is it ability? In truth, it is a culmination of things which cannot be isolated or fully understood without integrating backgrounds and environments into the explanation. You obviously were taught the importance of an education and had the opportunity to get that education. There are brilliant people everywhere who were not so fortunate.

It is dreadful when the educated look down upon the uneducated. This is shortsighted and egotistical. Not everyone can afford college. Some people have rather miserable backgrounds in which education was not a priority. Rather than looking down upon the less educated persons, why not seek to find out if anyone would like to go to college and help them get there? Give a hand to those who did not have the support that you did. Be for them what others were for you. Perhaps, with a little encouragement, you can make an invaluable contribution to the life of another.

Seek opportunities to maximize the use of corporate funded programs like tuition reimbursement. Just because it is in the policy book does not mean that everyone will step up to claim it. In your dealings with employees, you will learn about those who would love to return to school. Help them. Some people need a boost of encouragement to take the leap to return to school. Offer it. If your company has unused benefits, shame on you.

As much as you like having some flexibility, have you not considered that others may also appreciate it? The world does not operate on rigid rules. As the saying goes, "Where there's a will, there's a way." Make great things happen. You have the knowhow and the tools with which to make amazing things happen. When you and your management team work together, you can create a wonderful working environment. Having happy employees makes a huge difference overall.

Chapter 22 - When All Else Fails

If they gotta go, they gotta go. But, let this be your last resort. Make every reasonable effort to retain valuable employees. Be honest about every employee and give every employee the benefit of the doubt. Try to get to the root of the problem before drawing conclusions. Examine all sides of the issue and do be fair. Just because someone made a mistake in the past does not mean that a mistake was repeated. Every incident should stand on its own. Don't try to string separate events together into one huge event.

I realize that you can't save them all. There are those who do not choose to be saved. You cannot make someone "get on board," even with your best efforts and intentions. Some people are simply instigators and love to stir the pot. Once found out, they usually either try to be more sneaky or they know the gig is up and change their behavior.

Have you ever noticed that "a bit dog hollers?" The guilty party will do amazing things to get out of the mess they've created. There are no limits to the measures to taken to avoid the consequences of actions, if deemed unpleasant. No one is safe from distracting accusations and blame shifting. The truth seems to fly out the window when guilt comes home to roost.

Chapter 23 - In The Best Interest Of All Concerned

When considering all things HR, one must look at all affected aspects of the actions and reactions of Human resources professionals. Up the ladder and down the ladder, the effects are all encompassing. The HR is organizationally vital and can help or hinder all operations. Understanding the importance of the human resources department can give you the insight needed to best utilize one of the most helpful resources available.

Upper management must allow HR to be what it was intended to be. It should not be a tool for use against employees. It should and must be a tool for the positive use of managers and employees. Today, there is much "talk" about open door policies. The harsh reality is that when an employee is duped into believing that there really is an open door policy as described in most corporate policies, the employee will come to sorely regret it.

Open door policies are, in truth, meant to be a snitch's avenue to the bosses. Bosses want to know who is causing trouble, so naturally an "open door" would offer the perfect guise under which to get to know what's really going on in the business. "Parking lot meetings" are the employees alternative to keep abreast of the latest workplace happenings. In yester-years, these meetings were referred to as "water cooler gossip."

Were manager to offer an honest open door policy, with no hidden retaliation, he/she would actually find this a truly useful tool to be able to get to better know the employees. How can camaraderie be improved when there is no actual open and honest communication between the parties? How can you relate to your staff if you know them not?

Communication is key to most aspects of life. As with your family, your workplace family also depends upon honest bilateral communication. Your boss cannot help you if he/she does not know that you need help. Similarly, you cannot know what the boss really needs unless you are told. But, communication will do nothing but harm if it is intended for harm. Honesty is the best policy, in fact the only policy which will optimize personnel performance.

Chapter 24 - Employee Satisfaction Pays Dividends

A happy employee will work diligently to promote the business. A happy employee will offer the best possible service to the customers. A happy employee will help other employees. A happy employee will offer you the best bang for your buck.

A disgruntled employee will cost far more than just his payroll. Sure, things break, but around a disgruntled employee, things break more often or get lost. Employees can "accidentally" drive a forklift into your merchandise or property. Employees can leave the water running to up your power bill. Employees can do all sorts of expensive punishments for your behaviors. You would be wise to realize this and behave appropriately.

You cannot win them all and you can't please everyone. But, if you manage to only make one mad, then the rest of the happy employees will help cover your mistake. If you make most of them mad, then who'll help you? Your behavior matters. You are expected to behave in the best interest of the employees and employers. This is difficult, but it is your skill that gives you the winning edge. Challenges are faced, but solutions can be found and brought to bear.

Just as in all of life, the many outweigh the few. The corporate managers must have the support of the employees to be successful. This must be understood and be the basis of the overall operation. One bad manager can bring down lots of employees, but one employee cannot bring down the entire organization. But consider this, several employees can bring the corporation down even further – it's called "class action lawsuit". Play the odds and err on the side of the masses. A building full of happy employees will cover the ire of the corporate bosses.

Employees have a right to work in an environment that is conducive to their overall productivity and well-being.

Corporations must ensure that employees know their rights as employees and provide a rational explanation for policies and procedures that affect them. Employees have a right to have all matters concerning them managed within standards that are both ethical and legal.

Chapter 25 – Now What

We have discussed the problems, now it's time for the solutions. There are solutions and we will explore the possibilities. We have seen the light and it has shown us a dismal picture. But, true to form, I do not believe in giving up even when faced with overwhelming truth.

If the entire game is rigged, how can we change the rules? The few versus the many, just as it happened during the American Revolution. The masses demanded their rights and stood for nothing less. This is the foundation of our strength and the basis upon which our rights must be restored. Together we stand for nothing less than the best that our profession offers.

I submit to you that the solution involved employees, corporations and Human resources professionals. All must make an effort to invoke real change.

My fellow Human resources professionals, we must lead the way. We must put the "human" back in HR. After all, we are the builders, the shapers and the safeguards for our corporations and our employees. We made a decision that HR is what we wanted to do. Now, we must take back our profession and not allow those in corporate America who have their own agenda to destroy the very foundation in which we are built on – ethics, morals, and values – the truth will set us free. Consider this, are you committed to standing up for what's right even when faced with adversity? If you can affirmatively answer this, then you are committed to positive change.

Corporations you must allow the backbone of your company, the HR professional to coach, lead and guide you. Isn't this the reason you hired Human resources professionals. Situations are often presented to us that we may not agree with or understand. You must trust the trusted advisors that you put into place. More importantly, cherish the absolute fact that "employees are your most valuable asset." You must treat them with love, dignity and respect. Like a child you love unconditionally but you correct when needed. Honestly listen to them and be open and committed to making real improvements and changes. Even the dumbest amongst us can see through insincere acts. Take your mission statements and visions for the company seriously. Read it and ask yourself are we really living the words?

CEOs and other high ranking officials, most of your massive workforce don't even know you are a real person. Sure, they've seen your name, but they've never seen you. You sit in your beautiful office at the corporate office while your workforce is struggling in the field being mistreated and abused by your management team. The very people you choose to lead your locations. I submit to you, step out and make surprise visits, talk to the people and they will talk to you. After all, if it weren't for these lowly workers your corporation would not exist. Finally, help your management teams be better managers, provide them training and resources to improve the communications skills. Stop empowering them to do the wrong thing.

Employees, invest in yourself, improve your skills and always do your best work. Follow company policies and procedures and utilize proper protocol.

There are no simple solutions or quick fixes, but one thing is certain, these are win-win solutions for everyone.

Chapter 26 – Options Reviewed

Aside from joining forces, what really are our options for resolution? How can we put the "human" back into the corporation and HR? How can we restore humanity to the heartless organizations in which we now must serve? As the eternal optimist, I do still believe that we can, relatively quickly, with the willingness and efforts of the masses, make where you work a thing of pride.

When asked where do you work, are you proud or ashamed? Were all Americans asked to honestly answer this question, what percentage do you think would answer that they are ashamed? I do believe that after all of the downsizing and cost reductions, most Americans are below what they would consider worthy of pride. With so many out of work and so many underemployed, how can but a few answer truthfully that they are proud of their current positions or the current company? For most, working is merely a necessary evil.

Most employees do not seek handouts. We want honest wages for honest work. We seek to be able to find work that matches our skill sets. We wish to be able to put our degree to work, so that we can repay our student loans.

There are always options, even unto death. But which options are realistically attainable? How do we go about resolving our problems when there are so few "extra" resources available?

What is one of the most available resources that we currently have? The unemployed are available and able to do much to transform America. There are some truly intelligent and gifted persons who are desperate for the opportunity to make a difference. How do we rally the troops?

Speaking of troops, there are lots of unemployed troops which are highly skilled and available to do whatever is needed to get back to the basics. Why aren't corporations taking advantage of this untapped market?

It seems as though more and more corporations are looking for ways to weed people out. Background checks, drug checks, reference checks, etc. etc. I certainly agree that we all want to be in the safest environment possible, but due to what I have personally witnessed, I know that these precautions are not done out of care or concern for safety. They are done to weed out certain groups of people. I am more than certain that even the highest ranking officials would not be employed if random drug checks, background checks and reference checks are done. And, while I'm on the subject, it is a fact that more employees who are in "white collar" jobs commit unethical acts to get their position. They inflate their resume, doctor their references and lie their way to the top. So, how they sit in judgment of others when they themselves do what they do to get a job? He who is without sin let him cast the first stone, as the famous saying goes.

Chapter 27 – Strategy Developed

Now that we have the recommendations, we must plan our work and work our plan. So, who'll be in charge? This is usually where trouble starts. Egos run rampant and tempers flare. Leaders want to lead and followers are hard to find.

Our best human resources skills will surely be put to the test. This is a giant undertaking and must be supported by the masses or it will be crushed by the corporate bosses. We watched as the Occupy movements were slowly crushed under the weight of police brutality. Protesters were squashed like ants under the weight of the forces amassed against them. Quickly and quietly they dissolved into a faint memory.

Yet, behind the walls of corporate America, the proud heart still beats.

Chapter 28 – Plan Implemented

Man your stations, as it were. Everyone to his/her post for the all out assault on inhuman and unfair corporate practices. We demand our rights and are determined to once again know what is like to depend upon your company while your company depends upon you. Although I have never witnessed this concept, I remain hopeful nonetheless.

Chapter 29 – Results Monitored

The best laid plans. We all make them and are very determined to see them through. We work diligently to carefully layout the intricate details of our most well thought out plans. We lay awake at night, losing sleep, so that we will feel completely prepared for the day ahead. But, no sooner than our day starts, we then realize that we are off our predetermined schedule. All our plans have gone awry.

So, now we have to reevaluate our day, constantly living on the fly with our minds boggled with unplanned for events. At the start of the day, we are bombarded with "must do's" that take us completely off our path. We are met with absences and shortages and problems to be fixed. When all of these issues are addressed, the bulk of the day is gone. Then we can now turn our attention to the regular stuff, like hiring and firing.

With the complaints out of the way, we can get on to the mountain of paperwork that goes with the hiring/firing daily duties of the one who thought he/she was hired to support the organization by soliciting and hiring the most qualified and hard working associates who will make long term careers with the company. There will be no time allotted for hiring/firing as happy employees stay till retirement, right?

The current rate of corporate employee turnover is staggering, to say the least. The never ending turnover keeps the revolving door turning so fast that the whirlwind caused by it can cool the lobby. The happy human resource professional is slowly worn down from the shear stress of simply watching the comings and goings of staff. There seems no end and no amount of effort or research will guarantee the success of a candidate for hire. There is no science which will ensure employee satisfaction.

Chapter 30 – Analysis Analyzed

Hindsight is twenty/twenty vision. Looking back, you see things more clearly. It is now easier to understand how things have gotten to this point. You can now see how the vice of profit maximization slowly clamped down on the numbers of employees. You see now that there was clearly a deliberate plan in place to downsize employer payrolls to maximize efficiency and profits. It was never about anything but this – the bottom line.

Corporate greed created the "Great CEO's" who have liquidated corporations and have only temporarily improved profits at the long term expense of all involved. The outside CEO's are hired, knowing nothing about the business and caring even less about employees. They are there to do one thing which is to get stock prices artificially high so that stocks can be sold at the highest possible prices. Once the top owners have sold their stock, the bottom falls out on the employees. The Great CEO has taken his/her golden parachute to retirement happiness or maybe even the next liquidation success.

Having watched as earned vested retirements are stolen, the heartbreak of American workers is rampant. After having given so much for so many years to have it all simply taken is one of the greatest injustices upon our homeland. Of course, after so many farmers and homeowners have lost their ancestral lands and homes, are we really surprised? Now that most of our farms are operated by corporations, surely they do not care about the GMO crops that earn them the highest possible yields per acre. Another win for corporate America.

Another loss for the employees in corporate America.

Chapter 31 - Remediation Recommended

When you take your car to a mechanic, you tell him/her what's wrong and he sets about figuring out the problem or at least making a best guess he/she then gives you a recommendation for remediation. You either choose to follow it or offer another alternative for the mechanic to explore.

This is much like going to the doctor for yourself. The same problem resolution actions are followed, unless you are unconscious. Then, the doctor has to make remediation plans and follow them. In a life and death situation, recommendations are not often sought or needed. If all the employees go on strike, it's too late to avoid a strike. But why does the thought of a strike seem like a viable solution when it does not benefit anyone? Workers aren't getting paid and companies aren't being productive.

Many, if not most, of company problems could be avoided if you just simply listened to those whom you hired for their expertise. When we determined that we were the owners of employees and could treat them as we pleased, we failed to realize that employees are crucial to our livelihoods and success. A disgruntled employee can wreak havoc on an organization with one action. It is the wise among us who realize this.

Sure, you can ride hard over the minions and treat them as cattle. Yes, and many of today's managers do this and feel empowered in the doing. But, even in the short term, while the manager is riding high, a storm is brewing in the background that will surely soon come rolling in to blow up in the manager's face. Rather than taking the more ethical route, ego played its hand and demanded that the manager rule the roost.

It's now time to pay the piper. The entire organization is in chaos after the disgruntled employee walked in with a gun and began shooting people. No amount of regret or effort now will undo the past. The deed is done. Now the consequences must be faced and they are far more harsh than the initial source of discontent.

This is not to say that no employee should be fired or that inefficient workers should not be disciplined. In our haste to take control and keep control, we forget that we are dealing with complicated human beings. This is a grand mistake. Yes, you have the power and right to terminate an employee, especially in an at-will state. But, the law does not provide for the consequences of your actions. There are always consequences and not necessarily the ones that you had so carefully measured.

Recently in the news there was a story about a young girl who resorted to killing herself because she was bullied. The law so accurately deemed that her tauter should be punished. The same concept should apply to corporations, consequences for those in your organization who don't follow the rules. This includes employees and managers alike.

Chapter 32 - Responses Organized

With everyone's best interest in mind, the time has come to get to work on how this mess will be fixed. The problem didn't happen overnight and it won't be fixed overnight. But, the first step is the most important. Pulling together all the pieces of the puzzle makes the resolution picture come into view. The light of resurrection begins to dawn upon the minds of those who seek the restoration of our greatness.

As with any problem, resolution and listening is key, but only if what is heard is heeded. Annual employee opinion surveys are futile as Human resources professionals work feverishly to get employees to buy-in to the rhetoric.

The subsequent action plans become a pile of dust that is only reviewed the following year when it's time to do it all over again. Focus groups have become merely for show as none of the suggestions are ever seriously considered. A suggestion box is a complete waste of a box and what it took to hang it. Those who realize that no one is listening will fail to offer suggestions. The assumption that the masses are ignorant will result in the downfall of many. Even if they don't voice their knowledge, they have it and will use it when they deem most appropriate – typically in a lawsuit.

Those in power have for too long presumed the ignorance of people. People in their laziness and willingness to be easily distracted have allowed those in power to believe them to be ignorant because they do nothing contrary to this belief. Till one day the people's needs are not met and the point of no return is reached – then the sleeping giant will awaken.

Chapter 33 - New Plan Designed

Tying up the loose ends is how the pieces become the whole. With all parties agreeing to the plan, it can be implemented toward maximum effectiveness. Without majority approval, no plan will fully succeed, at least not without use of force. Most Americans pay taxes because they know the consequences of force if they don't. It is not about liking it or necessarily agreeing with all tenets of it.

No one likes all the rules, but for the most part, the rules are generally accepted for the good of all. We support our schools even if we don't have children. We support our military even if we are conscientious objectors. We, as civilized humans, agree to take part in this legal organization called America. We do this because we believe that it is best for those who choose to be a part of it.

Those who choose to work for corporations do so in a like manner. They believe that they are getting and giving something meaningful and for the betterment of those involved with the organization. But, is this really true?

There are those, who more or less, serve themselves only and do not consider others when making decisions. These are the minority and cannot usually sway the majority. But, they must be considered in the mix as they play a part as do other employees. There are employees who will sell out for a few dollars and will do whatever the boss asks. They have no motivation other than greed and/or low or no self-worth.

Greed is the master that makes the masses suffer. One selfish person can steal the wealth of thousands or even millions. The stories are too many to mention, but do you remember Bernie Madoff? Do you remember Adolf Hitler? Do you remember Fedel Castro and Papa Doc? Certainly you would remember the person who stole from you? It happens all the time and we need not stick our heads in the sand in denial. We must realize that this is a part of life and we must incorporate it into our plans, to the extent that we can.

I was shocked to learn that roughly eighty percent of corporate theft is done by employees, I personally experienced the truth of this as I watched employee after employee being walked out of the building for theft. I could not believe that some of my most revered employees were stealing from their co-workers and their families. Don't be fooled, employee theft is a great and present reality but then again we know from story after story that lowly employees are not the only ones stealing from the company.

Stealing is stealing and it is wrong, but consider this story and how society may have led to it. A working mother makes a decision to go into a supermarket and steal food to feed her children. She's arrested and convicted of the crime. Is this greed or survival?

What motivates someone to steal? The answers are as varied as the solutions to employee theft. A disgruntled employee may be more likely to steal, but this is not always the case. In human resources, we must know that no two people are alike and no two people have the same home situations or motivated by the same forces. An employee can be starving at home and you will not be aware until they are caught stealing. I've seen cases where employees come to work disheveled and obviously in some type of distressed. Everyone talks about it but no one asks questions or offers assistance.

Most large corporations say that they give back to the community but really who are they giving to? Why not help the employees who so diligently help you succeed. No working person should ever have to make a decision to steal because they don't have the money to eat although they are working for your company.

I am the biggest proponent that we make our choices in life, but I know from personal experiences that some regardless of their educational background or their skill sets are more fortunate than others. I often wonder if education truly is the ticket to good wages.

I don't want to take this discussion in another direction but facts are facts, some groups of people no matter how educated they are, they will never earn as much as their counterparts.

We all have gotten better, more polished, more savvy and a lot more understanding as the years go by. Why have we forgotten from whence we come?

Chapter 34 - New Plan Implemented

Over the years, people become jaded. People learn from their experiences and become molded into what they believe to be their reality. If a person gets robbed four times, they are more likely to believe that criminals are everywhere. This is not true, but the belief creates the person's perspective which largely creates their reality.

If you have more bad bosses than good, you are more likely to believe that bad bosses are everywhere. I have had my share of both, so I cannot say that there are more of one than the other. Within organizations, you can have both good and bad. If you find yourself in an organization which predominantly has bad vibes, you may do yourself a favor to leave willingly, before you are asked to do so. The cultural environment is very important and one must fit in.

Working in a toxic and hostile environment is awful and not to be taken lightly. You may have to endure for a time, but make up your mind not to stay too long. Stress affects health and working in a stressful environment will cause you to physically suffer. Do not kid yourself, you will not escape unscathed. There is much documented proof substantiating this. Suffering a heart attack is hardly worth the salary that you are receiving.

It is better to make less and have more peace than to work harder and damage your health. Have you ever stopped to realize that most people are sick today? Why do so many people take so many pills just to get through the day? This is not normal and is but one indicator of the stressful lives that we live. We are literally "sick" of working under undue stress. Company cell phones and laptops when does our work ever end. Have we really signed up to lead a never ending career life? The concept of work life balance is virtually non-existent. Working mothers and fathers cannot enjoy their kids and kids are raising themselves.

I applaud those companies that get it. They offer childcare services and many other resources that their employees may need. This undoubtedly ensures they have happy and productive workers. I can almost bet that these are those companies that on the list of the most admired companies.

Chapter 35 - Results Seen

A well-oiled machine runs smoothly and efficiently. An organization in which all parties are treated fairly and appropriately will run like a well-oiled machine. Employees are not unreasonable for the most part. They understand that the business is in business to make money. They understand that the business depends upon all parts pulling the communal load. An employee who does not have his/her heart in the business knows this fact; you mentioning it does not negate it or make it true to the employee.

Addressing inappropriate behavior or poor work habits with an employee is a dicey proposition. It can go badly or rather smartly. Much depends upon how the employee feels that he/she is treated. If the employee feels fairly treated, typically the employee will respond well. If the employee feels cheated, then there will be backlash.

Just because someone doesn't voice their gripe, doesn't mean that they don't have one. If you insult an employee who drives a forklift, you may find yourself with a very costly repair to the either the forklift of the object of the forklift driver's revenge. The cost to repair the damage can be very high. The time it takes to be nice is well worth the price!

I have witnessed a simple conversation that should have been done with respect and dignity caused the corporation thousands in a lawsuit. Preserving a person's respect and dignity is so easy. Yet this concept is not followed.

Chapter 36 - Intrigued with Relief

Have you ever noticed how some people are rude to the boss's secretary but are really nice to the boss? The secretaries also notice and they deal very carefully with those who cross their paths. Let's say you are rude to the secretary who books your flights. How long will it take you to get to where you are going? Let's say you are a boss who is rude to his/her secretary who is married to the person in human resources who prepares transfer orders. Where will you get transferred?

These things happen in real life and I can attest to this fact. Be careful who you are rude to and how you treat others. You never know what a person will do to get even. People do not see things from the same perspective. What may be innocent to you may really irritate someone else. As with every avenue of life, dealing with people is difficult. The entire organization lives or dies by the workings of all within.

All too often human resources professionals are treated as less important than other departments such as finance, marketing or sales. Let me be very clear – there are no completely problem-free organizations yet in existence. All organizations depend upon Human resources professionals. You will do well to realize this and keep it foremost on your mind.

Successful human resources professionals are the ones who have learned to strike a balance between employees and employers. They must be open and willing to listen to all involved parties and be able to offer fair and mutually beneficial solutions. There is no win or lose in this game. Both sides must win because there are no sides in reality for all sides are on the same team.

There can be no perfect solution for every situation. The realist will know and accept this fact. Another fact which will become more evident as you mature in your role as a human resources professional is that people want to be treated like you want to be treated. The Golden Rule is the rule for everyone to follow for success.

For the most part, people will respond in kind. If you are rude, they will be rude in response to your rudeness. You are the same, so you can relate. Put yourself in the other person's shoes and you will largely know how they feel and can more easily deal with them.

The longer that you are in an organization, the more you will come to understand the corporate operational environment. You will learn the quirks of the managers and how they prefer to do business. You will grow accustomed to working with and for all of those around you. You must not see yourself apart from the others for in truth you are a major part of the organization. You should seek opportunities to spend time with the employees as this will help you when they seek your assistance.

The better your relationship with employees, the better your relationship will be with managers, especially if the managers realize the importance of their greatest assets. Bob's Red Mill is one such organization. Bob, upon his retirement from the company he started, gave the company to the employees who had worked so hard to make the company successful. Now that's gratitude in action. He appreciated his most valuable assets.

www.ingramcontent.com/pod-product-compliance
Lightning Source LLC
Chambersburg PA
CBHW060413190526
45169CB00002B/888